The Amazing Real-Life Adventures of …

Whitey

For You, the Real Hero

Copyright © 2025 Steven Horne

This book is about Whitey. A Duck.

Whitey is no ordinary duck. He's not like the made-up characters you read about in other books ...

Whitey is real! So, the pictures in this book are photographs. Not drawings.

It's time to meet the hero of our story.

Here he is!! This is Whitey.

One afternoon, two of Whitey's friends were chatting. Deborah is the brown duck. David is grey and brown with a green head.

David and Deborah started bickering about what they were going to have for tea. So, Whitey went to play.

While Whitey was splashing about, he looked at his reflection in the water. But saw something else.

He looked up.

And saw a magnificent swan flying overhead.

Whitey waved his wings to say "Hello."

But the swan didn't see him.

When Whitey got back David and Deborah were arguing about what time to have tea.

Whitey interrupted, "I've decided to become a swan," he said.

"Ha, ha," David and Deborah laughed. "You can't be a swan," said David. "Just because you're white," added Deborah, "anyway YOU'RE too small."

Whitey had made up his mind, so off he swam with a "quack" and a smile on his bill. To start his adventure.

He saw a Cormorant.

A funny looking big black duck with a large, hooked tip bill. "Hello Mr Cormorant," said Whitey, "lovely day."

"It most certainly is," replied the cormorant. And Whitey stopped for a chat.

"I'm going to be a swan," said Whitey.

"The hardest part of fulfilling your dreams is deciding what you really want. So, you're off to a terrific start. Good luck Whitey." Said the cormorant, whose name is Colin.

He also made friends with a Heron.

A tall, skinny duck with very long legs and a bill like a spear.

"Nice haircut," said Whitey when he saw the strands of feathers round the sides of the heron's head. Joining together at the back to form a kind of ponytail.

"Why thank you." Replied the heron, as she moved her head with a swish. Letting the wind catch her feathers.

It was getting late, so Whitey decided to settle down for the evening.

He was a bit scared as it was the 1st night he'd spent on his own. But Whitey told himself it was all part of the adventure.

Besides, Colin the Cormorant and Helen the Heron said they would keep an eye on him.

All he had to do was give 3 loud "Quacks" if he needed any help.

When it was dark. Whitey looked up at the stars and saw endless possibilities.

Whitey wondered if there might be other duck-like creatures in space...

...He decided he would like to meet them one day.

At sunrise, Whitey awoke with an exquisite joy.

Today is going to be a fantastic day, he thought.

As if by magic. It seemed, no sooner had he opened his eyes. There it was! A swan. Swimming right past where he'd made his bed for the night.

Even though it was starting to rain. Whitey wasn't going to let it dampen his enthusiasm one bit.

"Hello Mr Swan," said Whitey. "Can I be a Swan?"

"It's not for me to decide," said the Swan. "If you can do what a Swan does, then you are a Swan. No matter what anyone else says."

"Brilliant," said Whitey. "What do Swans do?"

"I'll show you," said the Swan.

So, they set off together. The Swan in front. Whitey following along behind. After a few minutes, they met another swan.

"This is my wife, Sally."

"Hello Sally," said Whitey. "I'm Whitey."

He turned to look at Mr Swan, "Oh Quack," he said, "I forgot to introduce myself; I'm Whitey."

"Enchanté, delighted to meet you Whitey," said Mr Swan, "I'm Serge."

Serge said he was hungry.

So off they swam looking for food.

Whitey's neck wasn't as long as a swans. But if he put his bum in the air and stretched as far as he could. He could get to the tasty plants and insects under the water.

They started building a nest.

Serge told Whitey, "It's hard work being a swan."

But Whitey was having so much fun. It didn't seem like work at all!

He even found time to chase Serge in a game of 'round the nest'.

When all the work was done. They discussed what they are going to do tomorrow.

Over the next few weeks. Serge and Whitey became inseparable.

Serge taught Whitey to stand tall like a swan. Straight with a perfect posture. And to pay attention to what is going on in the water.

How to preen like a swan. So they kept nice and clean.

And how to walk like a swan.

Although Serge had to hide his face for some of the early attempts. So Whitey didn't see him laughing.

Whitey listened intently as Serge explained all matters swan.

But something was troubling him.

"I'm worried about Sally" he said. "She's eating and sleeping rather a lot. And doesn't play with us as much as she used to."

"Don't you worry," said Serge. "Sally's just fine. You wait and see."

It didn't take long to find out why Sally had been so preoccupied.

Maybe you can think up a name for one of the cygnets?

But not this one!

Who is called Fluffty McTuffty McSwanney Swan Swan.

If you look closely at Sally's back. You can see Fluffty saying, "Hello," to Whitey.

At first, the cygnets weren't too sure about going into the water.

Sally and Serge let Whitey tell them how much fun it is to go swimming.

They didn't take much persuasion!

Whitey spent the rest of the summer, being a swan! And having lots of fun with his new family.

Fluffty and Whitey would sometimes have a race.

He made sure the cygnets didn't swim too far from the nest.

They stopped for a rest when the cygnets got tired.

Taught the cygnets to find the best food.

Sometimes they'd just relax and enjoy the sunshine.

Time to get ready for bed. No more lonely nights for Whitey!

When they had grown big enough. The cygnets flew off to start their own families. Fluffty stayed the longest as she and Whitey had become special friends. But soon it would be time for her to go off on her own adventure.

Look at Fluffty now! She has swan wings, on a cygnet's body!!

It doesn't matter how big you are. It doesn't matter what you look like. It's what you do that counts. Doing makes dreams come true.

--- ---

Wherever you live. Go for an explore! Who knows what you might find?

If you find any ducks or swans and are going to feed them. Don't give them bread. They'll eat it, but it's not good for them. Bread to ducks is like sweeties for humans. They might taste nice, but they'll fill you up and not leave room for the nutritious foods your body needs to grow strong and healthy.

Peas are good. Frozen ones are fine, just defrost them first!!!

--- ---

It only seems right we let Whitey have the final words …

"If you want to be different. You have to do things differently. Quack, quack."

If you would like your very own Whitey. Go to whiteytheduck.co.uk

Printed in Great Britain
by Amazon